One Arm
But Not Unarmed

One Arm
But Not Unarmed

Suzan Nguyen

Published by
WSA Publishing
301 E 57th Street, 4th fl
New York, NY 10022

Copyright © 2019 by Suzan Nguyen

All rights reserved. No part of this book may be reproduced or transmitted in any form or by in any means, electronic or mechanical, including photocopying, recording, or by any information storage and retrieval system, without the written permission of the Publisher, except where permitted by law.

Manufactured in the United States of America, or in the United Kingdom when distributed elsewhere.

Nguyen, Suzan
One Arm But Not Unarmed
ISBN: 978-1-948181-35-8
eBook: 978-1-948181-36-5

Cover design by: Cynthia Lay / www.speakerwebsites.com
Editing by: Annette Craven
Copyediting by: Ayse Yilmaz
Interior design: Medlar Publishing Solutions Pvt Ltd., India
Photo credits: Suzan Nguyen, Patrick Hubbard

www.bbnbcoaching.com

Chapter 1

In 2001, my world turned upside down, in the blink of an eye.

Let me share with you what happened, to the best of my ability that is. I remember the exact outfit I had on that night–a cute, black, fitted top and some red jeans. A few friends and I were bored and decided to go out for a bit. We decided to head downtown to hang out. I was having a good hair day, and in my mind, it was going to be a great evening. I was ready to have some fun with friends—a spontaneous outing. It was a fun night, but after a few hours we decided to get in the car and head home.

On our way home, I was at the wheel. I remember talking and laughing when suddenly a car passed us and hydroplaned on the wet street near us, causing me to react and lose control of the wheel. The car flipped several times, ejecting me through the windshield. When I landed, a piece of the car severed my right arm above the elbow in an instant. The most insane thing is I actually do not remember anything after that flashed before my eyes.

Everything I am sharing I learned from others—doctors, nurses, emergency personnel, family, friends, and observers. I flew approximately 50 feet from my vehicle. I still cannot believe my body flew out the windshield and landed on the wet ground. I could hear my friends running towards me screaming and crying, *"oh my God Suzan, are you okay?"* I tried to answer, but nothing came out. I tried again, but no sound.

My head felt dizzy, heavy, and I felt lost and confused—lost for words and confused because I was not sure what happened or where I was. *How did everything happen so quickly?*

I do not remember much before the impact. I remember driving home, talking with my friends, and *bam!* That was it. Everything else that happened after was a complete blur. The next thing I remembered was laying on the wet ground. *Why were people crying and why was I laying on the wet ground? Why was no one helping me up? Why could I not help myself up?*

For the life of me, I could not even let them know that I was okay, because I had no ability to speak. Not only could I not speak, I could not move. How ironic that this was supposed to be the most painful moment in my life, but I could not feel a thing. My body was completely numb. I could not move my body, I could not open my mouth, and I could not even blink my eyes to signal anything to the people around me. All I could hear were the ambulance nearby, and the lights flashing. The people's faces were a little fuzzy so I could not see who they were, but I heard my friend Mikey's voice clearly—he was screaming, crying, and sobbing.

I knew something was wrong. Something bad must have happened. I started to understand there was something wrong because of the sound of everyone sobbing around me. This was going to be the longest and worst day of my entire life. I was already slowly dying inside.

Everything happened so fast. Everyone around me was panicking and seemed like they were moving so quickly. No one would tell me what was going on. I tried to make eye contact with everyone around me, but no one wanted to look back at me. I was so afraid, and my eyes were full of tears. *That* I could feel. They kept falling down my cheeks, but I could not move my body or arms to wipe them. I wanted to scream from the top of my lungs and wake up from this awful nightmare.

What the hell was going on? So many awful thoughts ran through my mind. I was rushed to the hospital where doctors mentioned that if the paramedics had not arrived when they did, I would have been in a vegetative state due to shock. If it were not for 60 seconds, I would not be here telling my story right now. It is insane to believe that 60 seconds could have changed my life forever. The thought of that continues to haunt me today. I have learned that time is so precious; we should never take a mere second for granted.

I vaguely remember the details but recall the commotion of the staff at the hospital and how quickly they were working so I could go through a variety of tests to make sure there was not any more damage internally. The doctors wanted to find out if there were any other injuries, so they had to put me through a cranial CAT scan to see if there were any other damages internally in my brain. All I remembered was being sent through a round tube that scanned my entire body. I was in excruciating pain. I will never forget the amount of pain I felt at that moment.

The scan viewed my injured body part from all angles. The scan normally takes up to 30 minutes, but for me it felt like an eternity. I remembered the staff wrapping my whole body in bandages; my entire body felt numb like it was broken into pieces. I felt helpless, and I had no idea what was really going on. The looks on the faces of the nurses and medical staff told me that I was far from being okay. I was praying that at any moment I was going to wake up from this horrific nightmare.

I remember when the doctors approached me laying in the hospital bed, asking me if I remembered what happened during the car accident, asking for details, I quickly interrupted with, *"Are my friends okay?"* For some reason, I was more concerned about their well-being. I knew I was still alive. Fortunately, they were fine. They had minor injuries but they were okay, unlike me.

Doctors gave me the worst news of my entire life; they were unable to save my right arm. I will never, in a million years, forget those words. It is insane to think how things can change so quickly, in mere moments. *How can one ever feel okay about accepting the fact that you wake up from an accident and no longer have your right arm?* Things were only getting worse and going down-hill from there. My new reality began as an amputee.

I asked the nurse staff for a mirror to check my face. I had tons of cuts and scratches all over from being ejected from the windshield. I was afraid they would all scar up because the cuts appeared to be extremely deep and it did not look good at all. My heart was breaking inside. I remember looking in the mirror observing my cuts, scratches and bruises all over my face while thinking to myself, *were any of them permanent scars?* I was wondering, *how ugly would I become? I am already disfigured, now my face is ruined too?*

I remember hitting my head, and my dad was so nervous that I would have long-term damage, so he pleaded with the doctors to continue to run tests on my brain. Thank God, that turned out okay. The only major damage was having my right arm amputated.

I was an emotional wreck, I was confused, and I was so vulnerable. I guess in the beginning, I was not processing what the doctors were telling me. I still felt and hoped I was in a horrible nightmare waiting to wake up. I was not going to accept it. This was not real. The doctors also mentioned that there was missing skin on my upper arm, at least what I had left of my arm, so they took skin from my thigh and used it as their skin graph. Doctors were doing things to me I never knew existed. I felt like a lab rat. I was lost. I was emotionally depressed.

I bet one of the scariest things that could ever happen for any parent is receiving that late night phone call that your child has been in a car accident and is at a trauma hospital. I can only imagine the emotions my parents had when receiving that late night phone call. When they arrived at the hospital, it took them hours to find me, as my name had not been processed in the system yet. My parents told me how long the drive felt from their home to the hospital. Normally it would be a 30-45 minute drive, but they remember their car almost ran out of gas so they had to hurry and go pump gas.

They mentioned it felt like the longest drive they ever had to take in their life. Their emotions were running high and they were afraid. The feeling of not knowing must have been miserable. They arrived full of fear, panicking, and running through the hallways screaming my name. Running room to room, crying, asking any staff member they saw: *"Where my daughter, where Suzan?"* (in their beautiful broken English). They still tell me how it felt like hours until they were able to find me in the hospital. It was the most heart-wrenching period of time they had ever experienced.

They finally found me in my room, wrapped in sheets from head to toe. Only my eyes were visible. They mentioned to me later that I looked like a mummy. They were afraid. They were not sure what to expect. I could see my mom at the end of my bed; her mouth wide open, eyes wide in disbelief and shock. Tears ran down her cheeks. She had her hands over her mouth trying not to cry or scream too loud. My dad was crying like a little baby. His body was trembling. He looked confused and afraid. I could hear and feel their pain, so I tried my hardest to console them, to let them know I was okay.

I tried to make things better, and the only thing I could think to say was, *I just lost my arm.* That did not seem to work. They seemed to be in more disbelief and became even more emotional. They could not believe that I mumbled those words. Now, their crying and squealing could be heard throughout the hospital halls.

It is unbelievable how your perspective changes as your life takes a dramatic turn. When did I ever think that I would be saying that I just lost my arm, but I am okay? I will be honest; fast forward from that moment seventeen years to now—it is still hard to believe that I lost my arm in a car accident.

In all honesty, my emotions completely shifted when I saw my parents. I was just happy to be alive. Seeing them made all the difference in the world. One thing is for certain, when your life flashes before your eyes and there is a possibility that you may never see your loved ones again, when you finally have that opportunity and reunite with them, it is the most powerful and gracious moment in your entire life. I was very confused, I was so angry inside, and I was depressed, but I was also very grateful. It was a complete mix of emotions. I was in a nightmare from which I wanted to wake up quickly. The emotions I felt during that time were indescribable. I was not sure if I still wanted to be alive or if I was better off dead.

In the beginning, I was praying it was a horrible nightmare and I was just waiting to wake up from it. I could not accept the fact that I lost my arm in an automobile accident. This just could not be real. I was in not only physical but also emotional pain. The amount of pain I was in during that time was immeasurable, and it was the type of pain I never knew I could experience or that existed in a million years. My family's love and support carried me through this extremely difficult time. I have friends who visited me and tried to support me as well, but during that time, I felt like no one really understood.

The staff at the hospital was extremely nice to me, and they treated me very well. I remember my mom coming to visit me and bringing stuff for both the medical staff and me. She thought that if she could do that she would be building a relationship with the nurses and they would take extra care of me. I remember the nurses checking on me, always making sure I was comfortable. I will never forget the way they made me feel. The medical staff made my recovery a little easier, and I knew I was in capable hands.

I remember relying on morphine to make myself feel better during my stay at the hospital. I was in so much pain it was unbearable. I continued to press that button so I could have some morphine. There were times when I was out of the provided amount, and I would be in such pain physically and emotionally until it was refilled. I would ask the nurse to do whatever she could to help refill it as soon as possible. That was the only relief for what I was going through.

To help me cope, the nurses extended visiting hours so my friends and family could be with me as much as possible. That was incredibly sweet and truly needed at the time. However, even though I had friends and family visiting me during my time at the hospital, inside I felt so empty. I felt like no one had a clue what I was truly feeling.

Chapter 2

I was at the hospital for a few months; when I was discharged, it was bittersweet. I still remember rolling in the wheelchair out of the hospital, and I was outside feeling the breeze in my hair and the sun in my face as I looked up at the sun and realized I was happy to be alive. In spite of this, I knew many challenges were ahead. I knew my life would never ever be the same. Thinking of the future made me sick to my stomach. This was going to be the beginning of a very long road. A few months later, after coming home from the hospital,

I hated looking in the mirror because I could not stand the sight of myself.

I locked myself in my room for months on end. I did not want to speak to anyone; I did not want anyone to see me in my current situation. I was ashamed; I hated my new physical appearance. At the age of 22, for every woman out there, it is supposed to be the prime of your life. This was supposed to be a stage in life I would enjoy the most. For me, it was the complete opposite. I felt like an ugly monster. I could not believe this was happening to me. *How the hell was I ever going to recover from this?* Nothing seemed possible.

I was questioning, *why I was still alive? Why did I make it out of the car accident alive? What was the purpose?* There could not be any purpose for me to still be alive. I isolated myself from everyone; I was in an extremely dark and negative period. I felt like no one understood what I was going through; I did not want to have anything to do with anyone.

I started obsessing over everything I could no longer do. All of the basic daily tasks were now an uphill battle. I had to learn how to do everything with one hand moving forward. *How the hell was I going to do this?* After 22 years of doing everything with two hands, life changed overnight. The days ahead of me were not looking so bright. I felt so discouraged, and completely depressed. At this point in my life I thought, *why should I be worrying about this?* Life was so unfair.

I remember the nights I would cry myself to sleep, having dreams where I still had two arms and was *normal*. I would wake up to find that piece of myself gone. I was going through some major depression. There were moments where I wanted to give up on life. I would blame God and ask: *why me? What did I do to deserve this?* Those thoughts ran through my mind every single minute of every single day. It was exhausting, and I was becoming extremely bitter. I was becoming a negative, nasty person. I was also becoming very angry. I was becoming an ugly, bitter person. Someone I did not recognize. I became the person I never imagined I could be. The old Suzan was happy, carefree, and full of life. The new one was very bitter.

So many thoughts threatened to destroy my mind. *Would I ever meet someone who would accept me for me? Would any guy ever look at me again? What would my friends think of me? Would people judge me by my physical scar without getting to know the real me? Was I ever going to be comfortable with myself again? Would I ever love myself again? Would I ever be okay by looking in the mirror again?* The answer to all of the questions at the time was easy—*NO, NEVER!*

These negative thoughts consumed me day in and day out, and it was extremely exhausting. When I was younger, I prided myself on my looks. Growing up in Port Arthur, Texas, I modeled on the weekends for a few clothing stores, and after moving to Houston, Texas, I was invited to be in a few fashion shows. I was actually in the process of signing with a modeling agency as well. I remember submitting my photo to *Miss TeenUSA* just for kicks, and I was over the moon when they responded. They wanted me to send in more information about myself. I actually never had the nerve to follow through, but at that moment, I was happy that I received a response from the committee. That was all that mattered. I was happy about my physical attributes. It was easy being me; I was carefree, and I loved my life. I remember how nice it was to be noticed and praised for my looks.

Being young and carefree were feelings I would never forget. I was on top of the world but that was all over. Those thoughts and feelings vanished. I was about to learn the hard way that looks can only take you so far, and unfortunately for me, I felt I did not have even that. I felt like I was deformed and abnormal. I looked hideous. I hated the way I looked.

So I decided to get a prosthetic. While other girls my age were out there shopping for the next designer purse or heels, I was out shopping for an arm. So many thoughts ran through my mind. *How are people going to look at me with a prosthetic? How was it going to work?* I became devastated having all of these thoughts.

These are thoughts no one should ever have to think about. I finally decided on a prosthetic, but for some reason wearing it made me feel like there was something still there. I guess I was mentally fooling myself. Even though I decided to go with the prosthetic, it was really just for looks. It did not move and I was not able to do anything with it. It did not serve a purpose, other than for appearance. I became a little confused about what I wanted.

How was I going to face people again? How was I going to look at my friends again? I would replay the night of the accident and ask myself *what if* questions. *What if I had taken another route that night? What if I had not gone out that night with my friends? What if we had stayed in a different part of town instead of heading downtown?* I would look at old pictures and reminisce about past memories, and I would cry to the point of no return. My heart was heavy, and my mind was not right. If anyone has experienced that combination, they know it is a recipe for disaster. These thoughts began to slowly eat me up inside. It made me more emotional and it made me spiral even more out of control. I became weak, lost energy, lost my appetite, and didn't seem to care about my life anymore. I didn't care to live anymore.

My mental state was very weak, and I had persistent thoughts of *what if* and *what could have been?* There were ongoing tears about how I used to look, and how I looked now. There were constant memories of the past. I could not stop thinking about how I was going to face the world now. I was 22 years old, and experiencing the worst scenario a girl at that age could ever imagine. I would not wish this pain on any other human being. There were times when I would wonder if I would ever be okay. All of those thoughts led me down a very dark path, of which I am not proud.

I wanted some relief from my reality, so I began to experiment more with alcohol and pills, among other things, to give me what I felt was temporary sanity in a world gone wrong. I was escaping from my reality. I wanted to feel better and not have any negative thoughts in my mind. And it did work, for a couple of hours, or a couple of days, but eventually I learned the hard way that after returning to reality the pain was only worse. The pain was still there and more raw than ever. It did not make things better; it only made things worse. I started to lash out and became even more bitter. I became more lost and confused. The pain was completely eating me up inside slowly day-by-day. I was beginning to hit rock bottom.

After being in the house for so long and isolating myself from everyone, some of my girlfriends encouraged me to get out of the house. After hours of debating, I finally caved in thinking, *what could be so bad?* Maybe it would be healthy for me to get out, socialize with friends, and try to have some fun. It was yet another bad decision. We decided to meet up with more friends, but I was still very shy and uncomfortable in my own skin. The thought in my head was *I am going to see friends who have not seen me since the accident*. The last thing they probably remember was the pre-accident Suzan, now I am back in public missing a limb and wearing a prosthesis.

The embarrassment I felt was unexplainable. When I was finally out, I kept asking myself *why did I even bother?* I was experiencing major anxiety. I was getting weird looks from people, and it was a horrible feeling. It was a reminder of how different I looked from everybody else.

We ended up at a bar, hanging out, and trying to make the best of the night. The next thing I know, an altercation occurred. I remember there was a group of girls, and my friends were bickering and exchanging words. It all went down-hill after that. There was a lot of yelling back and forth, and next thing you know, I felt someone coming toward me, so I reacted. I grabbed whatever I could next to me to protect myself.

During that time, my mind was not in the right place. I was already so angry and in such a negative space. Who knows if my perception was accurate? All I remember is getting into a horrible fight and the tremendous regret afterward. I cannot begin to express how remorseful I am about the turn of events that night. I remember the cops pulling me off some woman, and I was enraged. The police took me outside and sat me down. The police were wondering how they could handcuff me as I only had one arm, so they end up handcuffing my arm to some rail.

I clearly remember that detail because I remember how ashamed I truly was at that exact moment. I could see people walking past me as I sat on the cement handcuffed to some railing next to me. I could see flocks of people, pointing, staring, and speaking amongst themselves wondering, *what the heck happened?* There was blood all over my clothes and on the scene, and my prosthesis was practically falling off my arm. I was mortified and in complete disgrace. I was extremely embarrassed. *What on earth happened so quickly? What had I done? Why did I feel threatened enough to put myself in such a bad situation? Why would I allow anyone to manipulate my emotions that way?*

All I remember is the police asking questions and taking our statements. Of course, both parties had a version of the story. There are always three sides to a story—your side, their side, and the truth. At that moment, I kept thinking: *what was the truth? Was I still bitter and negative with a hazy perspective? Who was to blame for this? Anyone?* Regardless of what happened, I knew by watching the police take our statements and interview witnesses, and seeing the look on their faces, it was going to be a very long night. *How was I going to explain this to my family?* In my mind, I was telling myself I should have stayed home. Maybe I was not mentally and physically ready to face everyone just yet. *What on earth did I get myself into? Was I trying to prove myself for some reason because I only had one arm?*

I ended up in the backseat of a police car, and it was the most humiliating event in my life. So many thoughts were running through my mind. I will never forget what happened that night. I remember getting my mug shot, being booked, being fingerprinted, and ending up in a holding tank. It was the worst experience

I could imagine, but this was just the beginning. I was my own worst enemy. I had been at war with myself, and this was a true testament that I was on the losing side.

Walking into the overcrowded holding tank, I heard the prison doors slam shut behind me. That sound traumatizes me to this day. I still remember walking in and feeling very nervous and scared. As I walked in, all the loud noise came to a screeching halt. It got extremely quiet, and I could feel the stare of every single girl. They all stopped what they were doing and immediately looked up at me, and everyone looked extremely intimidating. There some women who were on the toilet handling their business while others were casually holding conversations with the others, a group of girls were arguing with each other while others were laughing without a care in the world.

There was so much going on all at once. It was such a small space, and it was crowded; everyone sat where they could find a place. It was filthy. It had a bad odor, and some people in there looked exhausted, as if they had been in there for days. I knew I did not belong there. Another memory I can't seem to forget is watching a woman start her menstrual cycle while sitting on the floor of the holding tank. Sadly some of the girls in there were pointing at her, making fun of her, and laughing hysterically. I was flabbergasted and sick to my stomach. I was having a slight panic attack. Although I just got there, I already wanted to get the hell out of there. It hit me like a ton of bricks, I realized that there were some serious repercussions in my near future.

The process took forever. I couldn't stop biting my nails and every horrible thought crossed my mind. I was waiting to make my one phone call but afraid at the same time. *Who was I going to call?* I was so afraid to call home and let them know what happened. *How was I going to explain that the first night I decided to go out and feel normal again, I ended up in jail? How on earth was I going to explain this to my parents?*

My mom was already very nervous about me going out with my prosthesis and not being able to take care of myself physically. *How was she going to understand what I had gotten myself into? Was I digging a deeper hole for myself?* First, I lose my arm and now I am losing my freedom. *What was God trying to tell me?* This had to be a sign that I am on the wrong path. It was clear as day sitting on the floor of that disgusting holding tank with blood on my clothes, breathing the staggering odor, and gagging that there had to be a message in all of this. I had no words. I just could not believe where I was. It was a never-ending nightmare.

I remember the food they served us in the holding tank was nasty. It was cold and tasted so bland. They served it in a plastic tray and just looking at it made me lose my appetite. The girls kept telling me to make sure I ate, but I did not listen. *How could I eat that food?* I remember the bologna sandwiches that they continuously served us. After a while, I got so hungry and my stomach was so empty that I caved in, and I ate whatever was in front of me. The girls were right. I tried my best to keep to myself, and prayed that things would work out somehow one way or another. I just needed to get out of there as soon as possible.

The entire process felt like it took an eternity. I had to wait my turn to see the judge first thing Monday morning as this happened during the weekend. It was the longest few days of my life. Making that phone call to my parents was hard. You could hear my mom screaming and yelling with extreme concern. When I was released on bond, the problems were just starting. I needed to find a lawyer, I needed to find money, and I was afraid. Fast-forward through numerous court dates, rescheduling of the court date many times over the course of a year, and a ton of money being lost in the process, the judicial system finally come to a decision.

I was sent to anger management classes. They made it mandatory for me to attend, and it was extremely humiliating. I remember checking into class where they would give me a sheet of paper with different emoticons on it. Each attendee would need to choose one, stand in front of the class, and tell them why we felt that emotion on that day. People would be sharing their stories about their anger, and there I was with the prosthesis feeling embarrassed and full of shame. I did not speak up and share my story, I was too embarrassed. *Why on earth would I share it?*

After attending a few classes, I made a stupid decision not to return. My head still was not on straight, and I felt like I did not belong there. I felt uncomfortable and ashamed being there. Not returning was terms for violating my probation. I was convicted of my crime and then sentenced to serve time in jail. I had just dug a deeper hole for myself. *How dumb could I be?* I clearly remember the day I was scheduled to surrender myself to the courthouse to begin doing my time. How can someone ever prepare themselves for this? How could I prepare myself for the next grueling months? I remember my mom dropping me off right in front of the courthouse, and as she watched me get out of the car she seemed to be at a loss for words and so was I. I felt horrible and ashamed. I was angry at myself. *What on earth was I thinking not to complete my anger management classes?*

I was transferred to the county jail and processed. I was booked as an inmate. I had visitation hours, I was wearing an official inmate orange jumpsuit, and I needed to get used to being there for the next couple of weeks. I must admit, transferring out of the holding tank and into the county lockup was a little better. It was less crowded, and I had my own cell that I shared with a roommate. The thin mattress on our bunks was extremely uncomfortable, and they would wake us up around 4 AM for roll call each morning. There were rumors going around that people were catching staph disease when showering, so I was so afraid to take a shower. I tried to hold out as long as I could to not shower.

Jail was a disgusting environment. The guard told me about commissary, which is an account that you can have set up for your loved ones to send you money so you can buy personal items in the jail store. Thank God I had friends and family who sent me a little money so I was able to do that. I used the money to buy personal items such as tampons and whatever else I needed to survive for the next few weeks. There was an incident when a woman in there tried to take advantage of me and asked me to buy her some items from commissary. She said she would pay me back as she was waiting for her funds to arrive. Being the person I am, I did. I went ahead and believed her but that was just a stunt to pull on the 'new girl' A lesson learned for me.

Another girl tried stealing my shoes but by then I was catching on that I needed to stand up for myself and be firm so I said in a tough voice, "those are my shoes". I still remember those shoes, they were cotton candy blue and so nice. It was a rough environment and I needed to learn that very quickly. I was told by some other girls not to be too friendly because that's how they see your weakness.

I learned a lot in there, and I definitely had plenty of time on my hands to reflect on my life. I had time to look around and realize that I had way too much going for me to be in that situation. I had time to reflect and made a promise to myself that I would never end up in jail again. That experience brought about a revelation about how important it is, regardless the situation, not to allow people to have control over my emotions.

I learned that we can be our own worst enemy at times, but we must prevail and persevere. I learned that I could no longer be my own worst enemy. I could no longer be at war with myself. I learned that no one is to blame for my actions but me. I learned that once you react to a situation, you lose control of the situation, your choices, and your options. I learned that I could not place blame or point fingers at anyone but myself for what I have done. I learned these valuable lessons the hard way.

I prayed every night while I was there. I knew if given the chance, I would be better. I realized that I did not belong in there. Thank God there was an issue with overcrowding, and because of the overcrowding, they ended up letting me out a few weeks instead of a few months later. Although I was released after a few weeks, it still felt like an eternity. Essentially, the judge was able to drop my charge to misdemeanor assault. I swore to myself that I would never ever return there. No one and nothing was ever worth my freedom. I would never allow any situation to control my emotions the way it did that awful night. I would never ever allow myself to get that worked up and angry again. Anger does not solve anything, but it can destroy everything.

Chapter 3

Now I had to think about moving forward. *How was I going to have a bright future with that on my record?* My reputation was tarnished. I was tarnished. I had let my anger get the best of me, and this was the result. I was more down and out now than I thought I could ever be. *What was happening to my life? Who was I becoming?* Losing my arm was making me slowly lose my mind. After this incident, I really decided to isolate myself. I realized that I had a lot of work to do on my own. I needed to get away from the noise, get away from everyone, and just look deep within myself. *Yes, losing my arm was one of the worst events in my life, but if I were to continue on this route, it would not be the last tragic event in my life.* I felt more alone than I ever had, and I felt that no one really understood what I was going through.

I began to become angry, full of shame, and an emotional wreck. I felt disgusted with myself. The emotions I mentioned earlier were hitting me but at about 100 times in magnitude. I was hitting a dead end. I had no idea what to do with myself. I wanted temporary relief to escape my reality and to feel normal again. But when the drugs wore off, I was exhausted, and I had to face my life again. It was so hard to handle. I was thinking to myself, *was there a way out?* I spent countless nights, locking myself in my room, with no appetite, no interaction with anyone, just being by myself and crying until there were no more tears. I remember nights when I would cry until the sun came up. I would cry until there was this horrible feeling in the pit of my stomach. I would cry until my eyes were nearly swollen shut and I had to put ice on them to relieve the pressure.

So many questions ran through my mind. *Would this pain ever go away? Why was it still hurting so badly? Why on earth was I still alive for this?* I finally had enough.

I allowed myself to be the victim and feel sorry for myself. In addition, I blamed myself until I finally decided that time was up. I could not do it anymore. My heart would not allow it, and my mind would not allow it either. After several months at being at my lowest point, I finally realized what I needed to do in order to move on.

It was not going to be easy, and I was not sure how I was going to do it, but I knew I needed to do something instead of allowing this horrible situation to take over my life because that is what it was doing slowly but surely eating me up inside. I started becoming afraid of my future. Afraid that I was not going to see another day. Afraid of whether there even was a future for me. To be honest, if I kept continuing on the path I was on, my parents were going to bury me soon. I could not live with that thought.

I finally reached a turning point; I still remember that moment very clearly. It was one of those nights I cried myself to sleep. I remember waking up and seeing the sun coming up, peeking through the blinds in my bedroom. It was extremely emotional, and it was a very powerful moment. I made the conscious decision I needed to be strong. I did not want to battle. I realized I had the choice to *be bitter or try to be better*.

I made the conscious decision to try my best to no longer be bitter but to be strong. They say you never know how strong you are until your strength has been tested. I can attest to that. I was going to fight, and give it my all, because I wanted to live again. I wanted to feel normal again. I wanted to just be me again. There is a quote I love by Isabel Allende. *We seem to all have an unsuspected reserve of strength inside that emerges when life puts us to the test.* I completely resonate with that statement.

So many memories started running through my mind of childhood events, and

I started remembering the times when I was very strong, when I was a tough little cookie. I started reminding myself of how strong I needed to be for this. It was the test of a lifetime. I told myself I could do this, I had to do it. *Did I have any other choice? What was the alternative if I did not try?* I was finally ready to run and catch up in a world that does not wait for anyone else. I wanted to be better. I wanted to be happy again. Although my definition of happiness would be completely different from many people I knew, I wanted to fight for it. I wanted to smile again, to laugh again. Although none of those thoughts seemed to be achievable in the moment, maybe some were possible in the near future.

I started to learn to do things with one hand that made me jump for joy. They were small milestones for me. For instance, learning how to use the wall to my advantage, I would be holding a hairclip with my teeth, then taking my hair and twisting it with my hand, then pressing my head against the wall, then using my hand to grab the hair clip from my mouth and clipping my hair—that was freaking awesome!

Slowly but surely, I was learning to do things my own way, to the best of my ability. I also learned to open a can of soda or a bottle of water. I would place it between my legs, holding it closely together using a little force, and use one hand to twist the cap. I was starting to learn how to do things on my own and did not need to ask anyone for help. Now, *that felt good!* I started to think how, in the past, I took so many things for granted. I started understanding and to really appreciate the little things in life more than I ever imagined before. The lessons I was learning through this were helping me grow in ways I never thought possible. I did not want to give up. I was going to persevere and try to live again. I had no idea that I was on the way to being a better version of myself. It definitely was not going to be easy, but I had nothing but time on my hands—or I guess you could say hand, singular.

Chapter 4

During my recovery, I experienced something called *phantom pains*, which is a sensation that feels like it's coming from a body part no longer there. Doctors once believed this was psychological, but have since discovered it is a real sensation that originates from the spinal cord and brain. It is the craziest sensation I have ever felt. Actually, even today I still have phantom pains. As I am closing my eyes right now and squeezing my right hand, which is no longer there, it really feels like my arm is still there. It is a wild feeling, actually. In the beginning, it was the most uncomfortable feeling to have. Sometimes, I thought that feeling would drive me crazy. I had to learn how to adapt to it.

I started looking for a job six months after the accident, because I wanted to feel normal again. I wanted to do normal things. It was difficult in the beginning, as employers would doubt my physical ability. I remember going with my cousin to a temporary agency to take a typing test for a job, and he was so pissed when I actually got the job because my typing skills were faster than his were. That moment was everything to me and gave me a boost in confidence. I continued looking for a job, and it was not easy but I was not going to quit.

I remember in the beginning my mom would drive me around Houston, all around town for interviews, and she was still amazed and completely shocked how quickly I wanted to jump back in the workforce. I was determined to be somewhat independent again. I was determined to start making my own money. I was determined to have social interaction once again, and I knew what I wanted to do. I was slowly getting to that point. I was determined to find a job and begin working as that was a part of my normalcy.

I had begun working at the age of 16 years old had always been extremely independent, and enjoyed making my own money. Getting back into the workforce was not easy, but I realized that there were many things I was still able to do, just maybe a little slower than other people were. I was still able to type pretty fast, people were shocked about that. There were many things I had to learn to do with one hand. Therefore, I figured out a way someone would do things with my situation. At this point in my life, my friends and family were still amazed at how I did things, finding my own way to get things done differently than someone with two working arms.

I have always been a hard worker, independent, and making my own money. Perhaps I could have looked into applying for disability, but I was not going to go out like that. I still had my other hand, and I still had my brain, my shrewdness, and the ability to do everything I did before. Well, almost everything and maybe a little bit slower than before, but I had to at least try. I remember my best friend Anna and I started working together at random places when we were 16 years old. She was the first friend I made when I moved to Houston. Anna was very protective of me. We made it a point to do everything together, and we were inseparable. We decided to apply for a few jobs together, and we were so pumped when we got our first jobs together. We always requested to be on the same shift, and when we started working together at places like China Coast, Schlotzsky's, and IHOP, we created some of the best memories together. I am grateful that we still share an amazing friendship. I cherish it deeply.

After I landed a job, I believe it was in customer service, my mom would continue to take me to work and drive me home on a daily basis. I remember my mom was so amazing during that time. She would do anything to try to make me smile again. After a couple of months of having her drive me around, I told myself it was time for me to start driving myself. Although it was going to be extremely tough because I was completely traumatized from the car accident, I knew I needed to try driving again. I could not allow that car accident to prevent me from driving for the rest of my life. In the beginning, I was very nervous, but after a few times on the road, I started getting the hang of it again.

It was not easy trying to learn to do everything with one hand. Not only did I need to relearn how to drive, I also needed to learn how to write again, because the arm I lost was my dominant arm. Essentially, I needed to learn how to live again, but I was not about to give up. I still have a hard time tying my shoes, so I have fallen in love with *slip on* everything. In my mind, I realized how tough life was going to be but reminded myself that I was tougher.

Chapter 5

My family was a huge part of my recovery. My mom would unwrap and rewrap my injuries with such calm, love, and care. Later she mentioned that it was the hardest thing she ever did. There she was seeing her youngest child in such pain, physically and emotionally, and there was nothing she could do about it. I remember my sister Teresa resigned from her job to be with me every single day. My family was with me every step of the way and did not alllow me to give up when I wanted to. My family was my rock during that painful time, and I know in my heart that I would not have been able to get through it without their love and unconditional support.

Slowly, I began to accept my new reality. I feel like that was the biggest factor in moving forward. My family helped me through those lonely nights I mentioned previously, looking back on my past, remembering the good times with two hands. I realized that I could no longer compare my new situation to my old memories. I had to begin accepting the new me, and move forward. That would not be possible if I continued reliving the past. It was not easy as I said, but I knew what I needed do.

It was extremely difficult for me to begin going out in public again. It took me quite some time to want to be around people. It was so hard to face old acquaintances and friends being physically different. I remember friends coming up to me and saying *"I do not know what to say,"* and in all honesty, I did not want them to say anything. I just wanted them to be normal, to treat me as they did before. I remember the way people looked at me, in the past. I remembered the way people looked at me because, I admit, I was an attractive girl. Now the looks I received from people because of my physical scar was devastating. Fast-forward 18 years, and I still get certain looks from people, but now I am better at responding. One thing I have learned, *if you cannot change a situation, then change how you respond to it.*

I remember something my dear friend Hiep told me that I would never forget. He was visiting from Austin, Texas and wanted to see how I was doing after the car accident. After many attempts to reach out to me, I was finally ready. We met up at a karaoke bar, Café Vy as I remember, and I was embarrassed, not quite knowing how to act. I felt so awkward and uncomfortable, not just with him, but with being out again, at my old stomping grounds, having a new physical scar. I was embarrassed seeing old friends too. As we were sitting down, just the two of us having a frank conversation, I remember asking him, *"Do you think of me any differently?"* He responded with a sincere look on his face while looking directly in my eyes, and said, *"I did not became your friend because of your arm. It was because of you,"* and pointed to his heart. His answer deeply affected me in such a wonderful way; I will never forget it.

After that conversation, I felt stronger. I felt like I knew I still had much to offer to my loved ones, and losing my arm was not going to change that. I realized that it was a new situation for everyone, and we were all learning how to deal with it. Especially me.

I needed to focus on myself now. I was in the process of learning how to do things again, learning how to write again, to curl my hair again with one hand, to drive again. I was learning to be creative and reinventing ways to do things with one hand. The biggest challenge was learning how to love myself again, but I admit I finally realized it was possible. *I'm possible!*

I needed more than ever to be surrounded by positivity and a strong support system. I do not think I would have been able to overcome what I did without it. I started to try to begin accepting my new reality. I wanted to begin *challenging my limits* instead of *limiting my challenges*. This was going to be an uphill battle but I was ready now more than ever. I would begin practice writing with one hand, which after 18 years still looks like a chicken scratch, but hey, at least I am trying. Seriously, sometimes it is hard to read my own handwriting. I was slowly beginning to be myself, but I was becoming a better version of my best self. I started to interact with friends again, and trying to have a normal life. Things were completely different, but I was different. I had to accept that.

It was so hard for me to ask for help in the beginning, because I was used to doing everything on my own for 22 years. Now I would need to have someone tie my shoe and do certain things that I was unable on my own. That was something I needed to get used to. It was extremely difficult asking anyone for help. I felt weak doing that, and it took me quite some time to learn how to ask for help. I try to add some humor to it nowadays, and I will ask people to *give me a hand.* Now I do not feel ashamed to ask for help if I need to. I feel like that was something I had to recognize, acknowledge, and understand.

You could say that my perspective on life was changing dramatically. At the age of 22, I was not living life like every other 22-year-old. I was growing up fast, learning more about myself than ever before. I was teaching myself things I never thought I would need to, and I was learning things I never believed I could. I was experiencing things older people possibly never would need to. It was a completely new life for me in which everything changed, and in the process, I did as well. I knew I wanted to be happier, to feel normal again, and I had to create my own joy.

Chapter 6

Things that made me happy during these times were different from what they were before. It was surreal how my life had changed. For example, when I figured out a way to clip my hair on my own using the wall, I was extremely happy. I was writing a letter and realized my handwriting was getting better, and that made me happy. When I was able to put toothpaste on my toothbrush on my own with one hand—that made me happy! *We must create our own joy.* I was slowly peeling back the layers, and creating my own joy from within. Maybe others would not understand my joy, but it was not for them to understand. It was for me to understand.

I began to retrain my brain and look at things differently. My life was completely up to me and no one else. I had to step back and be extremely grateful that I was spared in that car accident. That I was still alive, that I was still here on God's green earth and my future was up to me, nobody else. I was a different person, and I was okay with that. I wanted to be better instead of being bitter. I began to read motivational books, trying to look at the brighter side of things. I no longer wanted to focus on things I was no longer *able* to do but focus on things that I was still *alive* to do.

One thing that was still a difficult challenge as a woman who loved clothes and dressing up was figuring out my new wardrobe. *How was I going to dress myself in certain clothes?* Sometimes the sleeves were too short on a shirt and my stub would stick out. Other times, the sleeves were too long and I would have to pin one up.

I remember in the beginning when I used to leave the house, I would put on the same thin black jacket, and I would place the right sleeve in the jacket pocket to make it appear to others that my right hand was in my pocket. I was trying hard to adapt and trying my best to be creative with my new clothing style. It was not easy. It was definitely a learning experience. I shed many tears with that process. Often, I would fall into utter sadness having these issues. Frequently, it would get me depressed, but I was reminded of the conscious choice I made to be strong. I reminded myself that at least I was still alive to have the chance to get dressed and figure this all out. It has gotten a little easier through the years.

One thing I needed to learn was not to compare myself to other people or how things were before the here and now. That would get me nowhere. I had to stop living in the past. My dear friend Jamie once said this to me: *Some people live their entire lives reliving the past so they have an excuse not to deal with the present/future*, and that was exactly what I was doing. If I were to continue doing that, it would only hurt me and not help me at all. I admit, I still have my moments where I compare myself to others and think back and say, *before I lost my arm*, but in reality none of those thoughts matter right now. None of those thoughts would benefit me in any way. *At all*. I am still in the process of trying to remember that. My husband always manages to check me on that when I begin to feel sorry for myself in any way.

Chapter 7

My husband, Phu, came into my life in 2005. He is originally from New Orleans, Louisiana and belongs to a large family. He is the oldest with seven sisters, and he is incredible. His whole family is precious and he is blessed with a great support system. I refer to him as *my angel on earth*. I could go on and on about this amazing soul. We met through mutual friends, and the first night we met, I was wearing my prosthesis. He never looked at me in a strange way, and did nothing to make me feel uncomfortable in my own skin whatsoever.

In the beginning, he never asked me about what happened to my arm; he seemed not to care. He only cared about the person I was in my heart. He cared about what was inside more than what was outside. We talked and laughed all night, and it was very comfortable. He was on a road trip visiting Houston with some friends, and they were nice as well. He and that huge group of friends who grew up together from a very young age had an extremely special bond. They lived in the Eastbank area of New Orleans, Louisiana in a Vietnamese community called Versai as known as Vietsai.

When he returned to New Orleans, we kept in touch every day. I remember nights when we would fall asleep talking on the phone. We stayed closely connected moving forward. He continued to remain as sweet as can be, and I could not believe a man like him existed. I had no idea where our relationship was headed; I just knew that he was extremely special. What we had was very special.

It turns out that he began making that six-hour drive more and more often. He would have his bags packed and in the car on Thursday evening, so that after work on Friday he could drive straight to Houston to see me. I was lucky enough to see him every weekend for the next eight to ten weeks. When he would make that trip to Houston, sometimes we would stay with my girlfriend. Other times, we would rent a hotel room and have our own space. When he was able to, he would cook for me, and I was completely impressed with his skills in the kitchen. I remember one time when he made this traditional Vietnamese noodle soup by the name of *Bun Man Moc*, I ate so much that I vomited. It was so good, and I got carried away. Oh my God, I was so embarrassed, but he tried to make me feel better by saying, *Do not worry, I made a big pot and it is not going anywhere. Take your time in eating.*

Not long after that, we decided we no longer wanted to be apart, so he moved down to Houston immediately after. Our relationship grew stronger, and I was quickly falling in love. It felt so good for someone to accept me for me. I realized what a special person he truly was to see past my physical scar. I still remember getting that phone call one afternoon, and he said, *I am moving down there. I have my stuff packed in my car and I am heading down there now.*

In my head, I am thinking, *it has only been a couple of months getting to know each other*, but my gut told me that he was the right one. Without even telling my mom or my dad, I hung up the phone, packed all of my stuff, and decided to move in with him. We had no idea what we were planning to do. We knew that we just were not going to be apart any longer. We knew that we would be able to wake up with each other every morning moving forward. The thought of that brought a huge smile to my face. We knew that we no longer needed to have a long-distance relationship. Those thoughts got us through the concerns, and we knew we were going to get through this together. He quickly landed a contract job, which paid way less than what he was making at his old job was, but I never heard him complain about it. Not once did I hear him express any regret about moving because of the pay cut.

I had a job in customer service that did not pay too well, and we were both just getting by. We rented an apartment not too far from my parents, and it was our new home. I remember it like it was yesterday. Our first dining room table was a cardboard box with the writing *our dining table* on it. We did not have much, but we were so happy. We were together. Thirteen years later, he has not treated me any differently. I often tell myself that he treats me as though he is still trying to have an opportunity to date. Nothing has changed, and I am completely all in. Sometimes I feel like I need to pinch myself.

A very interesting fact that came out since we met is finding out that he is related to one of my closest and oldest friends, Nga. What a small world I tell you. Nga and I had known each other for so long that we were like sisters; now we were officially family. I was happy that she was stuck with me whether she liked it or not.

Phu came into my life at the perfect time. He helped me in my recovery, and I learned to love myself yet again. He never likes to take credit for anything he has done for me, but in my heart and soul, I give him all of the credit. He helped me smile and laugh again, he helped me love myself again, and he helped me become a better person then I have ever been. He has helped me understand the true meaning of patience. He is the only man I know who brings leftover bread to feed the birds at work in the morning. He is the only man I know who carries Band-Aids in his wallet in case anyone around him gets hurt. He is the only man I know who, regardless how bad traffic is on our drive anywhere, welcomes people to cut in front of him even if he is in a hurry to get somewhere. He is so selfless. He is compassionate, and the most beautiful soul I have ever met. I am honored to be his wife.

One of the most important things Phu did for me was to help me realize I did not need to wear a prosthetic arm. I had not wanted a prosthetic that could move, because I felt like I would look like a robot, so I was wearing it just for the appearance. At the end of the day, wearing it added a little bit more stress to my life. It was useless. Phu helped me rethink why I was wearing it. One night when we were hanging out, he asked me about it. *Why are you wearing it? Was it comfortable? Did it help me?* To be honest, I did not have anything positive to say about the prosthetic. It was so uncomfortable, and it was heavy. I would get blisters on my arm from wearing it. One day, after deeply thinking about the reason behind wearing the prosthetic, I decided not to wear it any more. It was unnecessary. That was a very profound moment. I am beyond grateful that Phu helped me realize that I was lovable no matter what.

I knew the exact moment that I wanted to be with him forever. He was at his cousin's wedding, and we were in a long-distance relationship so of course, there could be some arguments that were stirred up just because we were missing each other. We got in a little argument over the phone on a Saturday night while he was at the wedding. Next thing you know, over six hours later, he shows up at my girlfriend's house where I was staying in Houston and knocks on the door. He drove over six hours in the middle of the night just to make sure that we were okay.

He stayed and we hung out for a few hours, and had a late breakfast. He got back in the car and drove over six hours back to New Orleans that day. That moment made me realize how sacred his love was for me. I have never met anyone in my entire life who treated me that way. Having this emotion for this man after losing my arm and him loving me with my physical scar touched my heart in ways I cannot explain. I was so lost, but was found again. Thank God for finding me my incredible husband Phu. The lost and found is a beautiful thing; *we must all get lost in order to be found.*

Chapter 8

By this time, I was on my way to being the stronger and better version of myself, which is what I had truly desired. There were some crucial steps in my recovery that I needed to go through in order to peel back the layers and find true happiness from within. I learned these amazing steps from Udemy.com where I continue taking their classes.

The first step was identifying my true desire. The key is to ask yourself: *What are your desires, and is you desire defined by society?* Define your desires. *Do they hold weight?* Desire can come from our exterior world, and that may not be what you truly desire. What you truly desire may, in fact, be internal. Our desires sometimes come from the influence of TV commercials or advertisements, or what our friends may have. That can create conflict. Most companies use psychology to sell to our senses. Companies like McDonalds and Disney World spend billions of dollars to convince you what you desire. Rather than give in to external stimuli, limit and define what you truly want. Take steps to create a different reality. Define what you desire and find out if it will really make you happier. *Is your happiness from a point of desire?* Having a sense of your desire will help you reach your true desire and your goals.

The next step is to address limiting beliefs. These are beliefs that we grow up to believe are true. Explore and bring awareness to your limiting beliefs. An example might be that because you are a woman, you will never make as much money as a man. *Are any limiting beliefs taking away your joy?*

Then, develop a sense of awareness. Be in control of your emotions. If you want more joy, you must choose to experience it. Create, be aware, and manage relations. Direct your emotions rather than allowing your emotions to direct you.

Recognize your identity ego. Your identity ego might be keeping you from being who you are supposed to be. *Are you being authentic or playing a role that you are supposed to in this world? What is your true identity?* Dig deeper internally and discover your true identity.

Examine your conditioning. *How are you wired?* In other words, *how are you conditioned to deal with life? Do you normally have a knee-jerk reaction, or are you emotionally grounded?* We all have positive and negative reactions because that is how we are conditioned. Potentially, how we grew up influences how we believe we should be. Understand and recognize the triggers for your past conditioning. Break the pattern. Take time to recondition yourself. This is a process. Make time to make it happen.

Your current mood and emotions determine your reality. Embrace your emotions and move forward. Bring your emotions back to the present, to the here and now. *Be* in the now. Make a choice and enjoy the present. Try not to think about the past or the future. Be in the moment now, and enjoy it wholeheartedly. Only in time can we truly experience glorious moments of joy. You can choose how you feel. What happened in the past is no longer happening. Do not focus on the past. Worrying about the future or focusing on your past will block your present joy

Adopting an attitude of gratitude means waking up and being grateful to still be alive. Truly adopt an attitude of gratitude. For me, there were so many reasons to be grateful. I was surrounded by the love and support of my family. I still had some very good friends who cared for me and wanted the best for me. I was still breathing and able to enjoy the most delicious foods that were known as my favorite dishes. I was still able to create memories and enjoy time with my loved one. I was still alive to do so much. I needed to focus on the things I was still alive to do.

Stop comparing yourself to others. This was imperative for me in order to move on. I needed to stop comparing myself to others and their physical attributes. The more I did this, the worse I felt. Learning to stop doing this really helped me in my recovery.

Learning to accept my new reality was the next step in order to move forward in my recovery. This was the new me, whether I liked it or not, and there was nothing I could do about it aside from accepting it and trying to be okay with the fact that I was an amputee.

In summary, I needed to check my ego. I had to be in the moment and stop reminiscing about how or who I was before. I had to *be in the now*. I had to recondition myself to look at the situation differently. I had to recognize my emotions and mood and realize that my current mood determined my reality. I pretty much *reprogrammed my wires*. Just because I grew up seeing people with two hands and two legs and thought that was normal did not mean having one arm was not normal. I had to relearn that I was still normal even though I only had one hand. I realized that everyone's happiness is different, and this was important for me to learn. Every person's happiness is different, because we are all completely different people. Being able to accept the fact that my happiness was completely different from the next person's happiness helped me create my own happiness. Things that made me happy but might not give others the same joy included learning to drive on my own again, learning to clip my hair on my own, learning to tie my shoes on my own, and learning to dress myself without anyone's help.

I learned that my happiness was completely different from the next 22-year-old, I truly understood the power and meaning of creating your own happiness from within. *That was my goal.* I needed to continue creating my own happiness. Although other people could not understand my happiness, it was not necessary to be validated. I knew what made me happy. I believe that was a huge factor in order for me to move forward and understand myself. Peeling off the layers in order to create your own happiness is extremely important. We all have different feelings and emotions behind those layers. We must step back, reflect, and understand what connections are behind those layers in order to reach happiness.

Chapter 9

I was becoming the new Suzan, the better Suzan. I started working for an amazing organization. I was becoming more comfortable with myself. I started allowing myself to find humor in my setback. Although my family and close friends already saw that side of me, I realized that I was starting to show it to other people—coworkers, acquaintances, even strangers. Just to make them laugh and to forget about their own problems for a moment. I started poking fun at myself and making one-handed jokes, because I realized that taking that situation too seriously would not benefit me in any way. It had already happened, so why not try to make the best of a bad situation?

In 2017, I was asked to share my story on overcoming adversity at my company's national conference. I worked at a Mattress Firm corporate office, which had a great culture and great people. Every year they would have a conference where the leadership team would come together and reconnect. The two reasons why they had this conference was for the employees to fall in love with Mattress Firm or to remind the employees why they loved Mattress Firm. I would say that Mattress Firm made me better.

A man by the name of Cory Ludens hired me, and ended up completely changing my life. He is an amazing man who believes in my story and me. He helped me grow professionally and personally, and I will continue to cherish his existence. Being employed at Mattress Firm changed me and helped me grow in ways I could never imagine. I have made some very good friends there along the way also. I have grown to love so many people at that organization. Shout out to my Mattress Firm family that will forever be in my heart.

The company's national conference was my time to share my story. There were many times I was not in the right headspace and believed that I could not go through with it. I have always loved to write, so writing about my story was very intriguing, but it was not easy. Writing about this traumatic experience and going back in time and feeling all of those emotions again was extremely heartbreaking and tough, but I felt the need to share my story on overcoming adversity as I know many of us have our own battles in life.

Everyone has their own story, and no one's is the same. While different, I believe that we are all aiming for the same result, which is to move forward, to *be better instead of being bitter*. I decided to go through with this project and began writing about the darkest time of my life. Strangely, during my time writing about it, there were nightmares and really bad dreams. I remember waking up crying, thinking I still had my arm but it was really gone. I guess the pain really never goes away.

After writing about my journey—six months of many writing sessions, many edits to my speech, many rehearsals, and many tears—it was my time to go on stage. It was my time to share my story with close to 1,500 people. Some people I knew, as my friends were there; the rest were people I had never met in my life.

Thank goodness, my family was there to cheer me on and support me. I was extremely nervous, and the morning of the event, I rehearsed my speech and went completely blank. I felt the need to vomit because I was so nervous. As they announced my name and everyone cheered for me, I felt the love, and my energy completely shifted. Looking out in the crowd, I saw so many people who loved me and were there for me. I saw my family, who were so proud of me that I was going to take this big first step and share my story. I was going to be completely vulnerable and share the darkest time of my entire life. *That was insane, right?* Normally when any of us go through a traumatic experience, we want to move forward and put it behind us. *When do we ever want to circle back and share with the world how vulnerable we were and how weak we felt during that time?* I was going to do just that.

While I was giving my speech, it was such an adrenaline rush. I was at the highest high of my life. I saw tears from the crowd, some people were crying hysterically, and they were all engaged with my story. I added some one-handed humor in there as well. My speech was about 18 minutes long. I was told I took them on an emotional roller coaster. As I finished my speech, the cheer and clapping from the crowd was overwhelming, one of my proudest moments. The feedback was incredible. I had people running up after my speech, sharing their battles, sharing how they were bitter. They shared with me how my story helped shift their energy and make them want to be better. I posted the video on YouTube and currently have over 20,000 views. I continuously receive messages from social media how my story has helped people move forward.

I finally learned to never be embarrassed by my story, as it can inspire others. I believe I can help others by sharing my story and, although it is never easy, it is very therapeutic for me. I am able to share my darkest time with people, hoping it can help them in their recovery, that it can help them move forward and be better. This continues to help me as well. I still get extremely emotional when sharing my story.

During a speaking engagement question and answer session at *Girls Inc.*, one sweet girl posed the question, *"what do you do on a daily basis to remain strong?"* I completely lost it, I had to turn away for a couple of minutes as tears were gushing down my face, and I became extremely emotional. I got myself together and continued answering their questions and it truly was a successful event. I share that experience with you because I admit, honestly, it can be so challenging and difficult at times to continue sharing my story. I do it because the feedback I receive confirms that sharing my story is helping others overcome adversity.

In our life, when we go through something traumatic, when we are vulnerable, and find ourselves in the darkest place we've ever known. Most of the time, we just want to move forward and not speak on it ever again. I never thought I would be brave enough to be sharing my story but I realize that sharing my story can inspire others. That is the reason why I continue doing what I do.

I do not believe it will ever get easier, but if I can help at least one person in the room during my speaking engagement and give them the strength to move forward in their dark moments, then I feel as if it was all worth it. I finally feel like I have found my purpose in life. My purpose is to help people overcome adversity, and to *be better instead of being bitter*.

Chapter 10

After the incredible feedback to my initial speech, I started hearing from all over the country from people who viewed my YouTube video. Because of this, I decided to continue sharing my story. I could see that the affirmations from people were strong, and I was able to help them in some way. I was able to bring some light during their dark time. I was able to help them move forward and give them the strength to do so. I decided I needed to share my message, so I have been.

Another thing I wanted to do was to become a life coach. I wanted to help guide people to the answers within. I wanted to help guide people to greatness and to shift their energy, to move forward. I realized that I had coached myself through the worst time of my entire life. If I could coach myself through the darkest time that I have ever known, then I wanted to do the same for others. It was my calling. I had to do this.

After spending hours researching, I decided to register for some coaching classes, which I completed eight months later. When the school loan went through and I was accepted without any challenges in the process, I realized that this was what I was supposed to be doing. I learned so much about myself during the incredible eight months of coaching classes. The content was life changing, the people I met were kind and amazing, and we were all in it for the same reason—to coach people, to guide them to their own answers within. Sitting in class, learning and soaking up the knowledge, was such a great feeling. I realized that I was exactly where I was supposed to be.

Isn't life so funny? When did I ever believe that losing my arm, going through such a dark time, and feeling vulnerable would ever lead me to where I am now? I still cannot believe it when I sit back and reflect about it. It is insanely amazing how everything has worked out. I have opened up my private coaching business—*BBnB Coaching, be better not bitter*. I am determined to help people move forward, to shift their energy, to help them be better instead of being bitter. That is my quest in life.

I have landed some coaching clients and have thoroughly enjoyed being able to help shift their energy and move them forward. A man I currently coach has the world at his fingertips. He is an entrepreneur, he has a family, and he has a nice income, but for some reason he feels empty inside. He is a great man, but feels lost at times. During our coaching sessions, I was able to coach him through a five-step program. Another client recently experienced a traumatic loss. She was going through a very rough time, and I knew she was a very strong woman. During our coaching sessions, I was slowly able to help shift her energy to help her face the adversity and to become less bitter. The five-step program has helped her tremendously in this transition.

The final client is a man who grew up in a very negative environment. He was not shown much love and appreciation growing up, and that haunted him as he was becoming an adult. In coaching, we do not focus on the past. We focus on the present and moving forward into the future. He is slowly falling in love with himself and appreciating himself more. He is learning to give himself more credit for the things that he does well. He has been my longest client, and in the past six months, we have made some great leaps together. I used the five-step program with him as well.

The 5 steps I mention are used to lay the groundwork and set up the foundation for each client I coach, as their situation is unique as well as their adversity. We all experience situations completely differently, and we may react different to the very same situation. We may also potentially have different perceptions of the same experiences. People feel pain differently. We all mourn and grieve differently.

It is important to get to know the real you, what you dislike and what you love about yourself, and baring all pain. Express your true emotions. Dig deep within.

With that being said, the first session is known as the *discovery session*, and it consists of looking deep inside ourselves, exploring our core, and identifying the pain that resides within.

It is crucial you recognize that pain and openly embrace it to be able to heal.

Secondly, you must accept your current reality.

Accepting yourself, your life, and your reality is paramount in this process. At times, it is very difficult to accept the current situation, as it may be your permanent situation. (This was extremely grueling for me to do.)

Change is constant, and some changes are inevitable. You can only be successful and move forward if you choose to accept it rather than resist it.

You must work through and accept your reality.

This process in our 5-step program takes time and dedication. Many changes are involved in this crucial step and I am there every step of the way to help see you through. Once you can do this, we can move forward.

Next I learn what is important to my client. What are his/her needs? Desires? Goals? Identifying and setting goals will achieve tangible results and is important to seeing your progress. What are your goals? How I can support and hold you accountable for achieving these goals? It is also vitally important you hold yourself accountable as well. How badly do you want to reach your goals? Figuring this out helps you discover why it matters so much.

Then we explore any energy blocks that may be occurring. These energy blocks may be blocking an individual from shifting their energy and moving forward. Some energy blocks can manifest in your body and cause many issues and challenges. We can explore and identify them and see what we can do to remove them, some energy blocks may be harder to remove then others. In order to create positivity and success, they must be removed and you must be freed from them.

By this time, essentially, there should be an energy shift, or a transformation, occurring. The client begins to become amazed at what they are capable of. They begin to learn about the great power hidden within themselves. The clients begin to feel the effects of self-discovery, fulfillment, clarity and they are slowly becoming a better version of themselves. This is a long process, and it does not happen overnight but with love and dedication, it is possible.

Although much more elaborate details are involved, this is a condensed version of what my 5-step program looks like.

At the end of the day, I feel like the top three things that we as an individuals want is to be accepted, acknowledged, and appreciated. If we want those things for ourselves, we must do those things for others. I truly believe in giving to receive.

I've learned that one of the most important things is to accept people for who they truly are, and there is a quote by Bernard Baruch that I think of all the time. *Those who matter do not mind, and those who mind do not matter*.

The second thing is to feel acknowledged. At times, we might do things for people that we love or in general. In most cases, we should not expect anything back obviously, but acknowledgement for what we do is important.

The final of the three is to be appreciated. Feeling appreciated is extremely important to most people. We need to show gratitude for those who are good to us, who do things for us without reason, who are there for us when we do not even share that anything is wrong. These are the three As that I try to be mindful of and to show on a daily basis.

One of the ways I do this is to volunteer and give back with my time to others. I am on a mission to help other people—to share my message, my lessons. One of those volunteer sessions was a *Be Better* workshop at the Angela house. The Angela house is a transition home for women who were previously incarcerated. Their goal is to successfully transition women back into society after incarceration. Out of many places I did research on, I was drawn to this organization and felt the need to start volunteering here. Can you only imagine what these women have been through? My desire was to help them make better decisions after their time behind bars and to be better instead of being bitter.

Chapter 11

When I walked in to my first *Be Better* workshop, I was nervous. These women intimidated me. Some of them looked at me sideways, even though they knew nothing about me and knew nothing about the reason why I was there. I was not very confident about how it would go by the looks on their faces. These were some tough women. Their demeanor and the way they acted—they had been through so much in their life, and I wanted to show them that I genuinely cared for them and their future. I wanted to do what I could to help them. I wanted them to be better.

Regardless of the looks I received when I walked in the room from the women, or how hard it was going to be, I made a promise to myself to stick around. My goal was to make them realize that I was only there for them—nothing else. I only wanted to be there to help them in any way I could, to help build up their strength, to help build up their confidence, to help them be better.

It was not an easy start; easy is an understatement. I hung in there. I was teaching once a week at the Angela house. Slowly but surely, being completely transparent with them, helped our relationship. They could ask me anything, and I would answer. I shared my journey with them and what I went through when I lost my arm. I also shared my YouTube video with them. I felt a slight connection. The women started opening up with me and sharing how rotten their life was. They were sharing with me their battles in life, and what brought them to the Angela house. The stories were completely heartbreaking. I actually learned many lessons from those amazing women on strength and resilience. I tell myself that I am better because of that.

Many of them were on the right track, going to different meetings with their drug problems, finding jobs, and just trying to find their place once again in society. It was not going to be easy for them, but I was there to help them realize that they were not going to give up. Also that I was not going to give up on them. I wanted to stick around and really be there for them.

After several weeks, our connection was growing. Our relationship with each other was definitely getting stronger; they were some of the sweetest women I have ever met. Some of them were just big old teddy bears, with such good hearts. Maybe they just were caught up and were hanging with the wrong crowd or made a bad decision in their life, but at the end of the day, they were all good people to me. They were all good people in my eyes. We developed a very special relationship with each other. They were starting to mean very much to me.

Next thing you know, I could not stay away from them. I was seeing progress in them, and they were opening up and sharing more and more about their stories. They were also telling me how I was changing them and helping them be better. Hearing those words was music to my ears. I love them all. The women that Angela house have forever changed my life. I was so grateful that they allowed me into their life and into their hearts. I will never forget any of them.

I still keep in touch with some of them on social media and I have seen few other women in person. I try to stay in contact with them and they all know that I am here if there is anything I can do. A few of them call me from time to time, they will update me with how things are going and at times we would meet for lunch, I would take them grocery shopping, or do whatever I can just to let them know that I am still here for them and to help them in any way I can. A few of the girls from Angela House and I actually have plans to catch up during lunch next week. I cannot wait to see how they are doing!

Here are some testimonials from the women at the Angela house that really touched my heart,

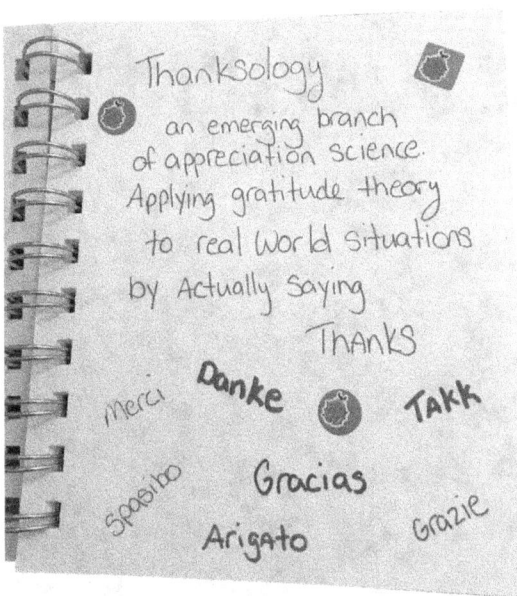

WARNING!

This book contains dangerously high levels of gratitude known to result in feeling appreciated and an increased risk of happiness. Please consult your doctor for a smile lasting longer than four hours.

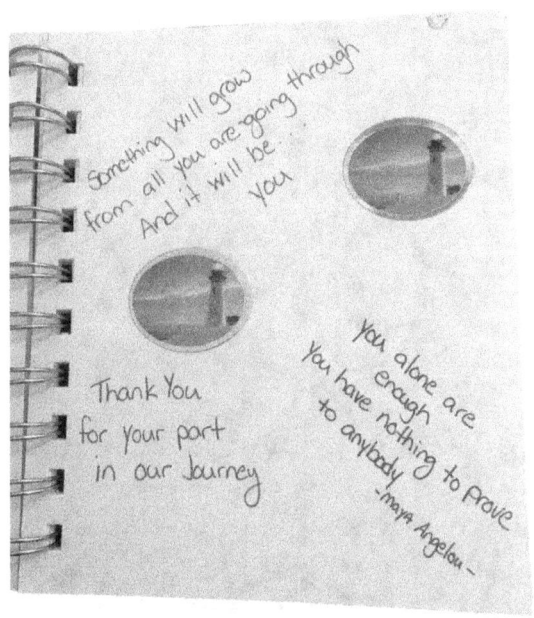

Something will grow from all you are going through. And it will be... you.

Thank you for your part in our journey

You alone are enough. You have nothing to prove to anybody.
— Maya Angelou —

What you've done & continue to do for us is beyond extraordinary. You give so freely & ask nothing in exchange outside of us to feel good about ourselves. I truly hope to be able to give back even half the amount that you do. Your genuine love & concern don't go unnoticed. You're a ray of sunshine during a dark time. There aren't sufficient words to express my gratitude. ♡ xo Abbie

(Venues)

My Sunshine

I thank you for the inspiration & the motivation you have given me. Love you for Everything. I love how you have given me hope. Beautiful & Awesome is you. Just as I was about to give up you showed up and truly I still stand!

Thank you Susan
for all of your
thoughtfulness and kindness
you are truly an insperation
May God Bless you
and Continue to give you
grace and favor!!

Your the Best

Audrey Green

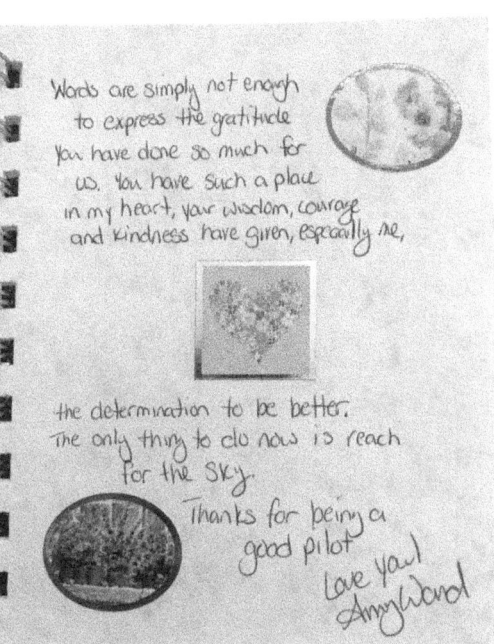

Words are simply not enough to express the gratitude. You have done so much for us. You have such a place in my heart, your wisdom, courage and kindness have given, especially me,

the determination to be better. The only thing to do now is reach for the sky.
Thanks for being a good pilot.
Love you!
Amy Wand

Susan,

 I Love You! You inspire me to keep trudging the road called life. You truly are a beautiful person inside & out. It makes my day to see or to talk to you. If more people like you were in our world it would be a much better place. Thank you for being you. I Love You & will never forget you.

Kristine

Suzan,
   You are absolutely a beautiful person inside and out. I admire your strength. Your story is AMAZING

I just love who you are. dont ever loose your will power. your story will help many, it just like it did for all of us at AH.

WE ♡ YOU
                    Amy Cantu

Chapter 12

You never know how many people you can help by just sharing your story, regardless how hard it can be. I feel like by doing that, it actually helps me out as well. Putting myself out there, unguarded, allowing myself to go through those emotions again just to be able to help others move forward is my purpose in life. In addition, it feels good when I am able to give to people without expecting anything in return. That is the best feeling one could give him/herself. I sit back and think about all the pain I have been through, all the tears that have been shed, all the hurt I have felt, all those lonely nights crying into the morning time. I sit back, reflect, and understand why I have gone through it all. I believe it is to help others overcome their adversity, to give them strength to endure the weak, to help remind them of how strong they are, and how resilient they can be during the time that they need it the most.

I am continuously looking for and exploring opportunities where I can be of help and serve others. I am open to any potential opportunities out there. Helping people is extremely gratifying for me. I find the act of serving others very meaningful and special. Giving back does not necessarily have to be monetary donations. You can donate your time, your talent, or your treasure.

Volunteering and helping others have many benefits to both mental and physical health. It can help counteract the effects of stress, anger and anxiety. It can combat depression, volunteering makes you happy and increases your self-confidence and it just makes you feel so good. There are many reasons why we should continue to give back and volunteer. Everyone can give something whether it is time, money, or some other way of helping those in need. I encourage you to step up to the plate and do what we can when we can.

I must admit I am at the best place in my life I have ever been. They say that nothing in life is coincidental; it is all in God's plan.

Having a strong support system is crucial during hardship. I do not know what I would do without that. I must admit, I remain very blessed to have a strong support system from my family and some incredible friends who I also call family. When I reflect on friendship, I think about the friends I have known for decades. In addition, I think about special friends who I have recently met and only had in my life for the past couple of years who have done more to support me, and to love me than they could have done in a longer amount of time. Without the support from my friends and family, I do not think that overcoming what I did would have been possible.

I have learned that there are some friendships in my life that did not work out; however, some people are not meant to be a part of your story. I have learned that some people come into your life at different times depending on what it is for. Some people come into your life so they can learn from you or vice versa: so you can learn from them. Others are here to deliver a message. Like they say, some friends are seasonal and some are forever.

Before, I would get emotional when I would lose friends, and I also would beat myself up because I felt like I was still in the process of learning about me and I made my mistakes. I may have said the wrong things, or expressed my emotions inaccurately, but now I feel like the lessons I have learned with people have really made me better. Without the mistakes I made, without the lessons I have learned, I would not be the person I am now, and I feel that wholeheartedly. I am better because of the mistakes I have made, the friends I have lost, and the relationships that no longer exist. I appreciate and love the ones who have really stuck by my side through it all. They are the real ones, You know who you are.

Another thing I believe is once you go through something dramatic in your life, and when you are able to heal and learn from it, it has made you stronger. We must share those lessons with others, because it is a gift. When we are able to share those lessons and the heartache—that is true strength. We in turn give strength and hope to the people who need it the most. We help them persevere and become resilient. My vision is to continue inspiring others. Whether through my book, my coaching sessions, my speaking engagements, my podcasts, or my relationships that I hold very closely to my heart, I realize what my purpose in life is, and I must admit, it feels really good to know that.

Another quote from Roy T. Bennett that spoke to me: *"Some things in life cannot be taught; they must be experienced. You never learn the most valuable lessons in life until you go through your own journey."* Yes, my journey was hard and at times I wanted to give up but I am so happy I did not give up although at times it seemed like the easier way out. Who knew life would be even better after losing an arm? My heart is full of gratitude and my life is full of joy.

I feel like I have become more expressive throughout the years. I have learned that nothing is a guarantee in life—not even tomorrow, not even with the people, you love... so I say what I want and express how I feel. It is not *what* you say; it is *how* you say it. There is always a nice and respectful way of saying something. I truly live in the moment, and I wear my heart on my sleeve. Many would say I am an open book, and clearly, I have nothing to hide. I have been through the lowest of lows, and I have experienced the highest of highs. I will never forget something my very dear friend Huy once told me. He said, *When God made you, he broke the mold*. I will never forget that and I couldn't agree more. To have a friend like Huy, is like having a thousand friends. That's how I started off my 'Best Man' speech at his wedding. Yep, you heard that right. We have such a unique and genuine friendship. I am blessed we are in each other's life.

I remember how it felt to be torn down and be at the lowest point, so I feel it is my purpose to help lift people back up and make them feel beautiful as they truly are.

We never know what people are going through, we all have our own battles in life. My physical scar may be obvious to the world, but there are people who are walking around without a physical scar and are hurting inside. Please be kind and gentle with everyone around you, as we might never know what battle they are fighting.

It has taken me a very long time, but as I mentioned before I have found humor in my setback. In the beginning when I lost my arm, I got offended anyone asked what happened as I felt it was a personal situation and I was not ready to share with anyone. After many years, I have learned with my story has helped others. I am able to laugh at myself, and have been very creative with one-hand jokes. For example, I always get half off at the nail salon. Why would I pay full price? Many people continue to ask me if I really get a discount. I have learned to not take life so seriously. What happened to me was horrible and a very unfortunate circumstance. However, I have learned to step back and 'reframe' (which is a very powerful coaching tool I use on a regular basis) and am always grateful that I am still here on God's green earth.

**Reframing allowed me to look at my situation in a different perspective, I continue to focus on the valuable lessons I've learned from it which made me become more resilient then I would have ever been in a million years.

I must admit, one thing that I am still facing challenges with is getting those awful looks/stares from strangers. I have experienced many times when the looks I received completely ruined my day. It used to make me extremely sad and made me feel horrible inside. To be honest, I still feel like that at times but I have become a little stronger. I realize that as humans, we are just naturally curious, and most people do not mean any harm. However, some not only look at me once, but also will continue to stare and make it obvious, which makes me feel very uncomfortable. My husband is great at helping me realize that I should try my best to not allow anyone affect my feelings. He reminds me of my strength on a daily basis and always makes me feel like I am the most beautiful girl in the room.

Reinventing myself and creating a new outlook on life took time, dedication and love. It did not happen overnight. It was a process and it took practice. It is extremely hard work but if you want something bad enough you will go after it with all you've got. That's exactly what I had to do. I believe in life, anything can happen with my four beliefs—BBPP. Be kind, believe in yourself, put in work, and pray.

I still remember like it was yesterday how bitter I was becoming after losing my arm. The negativity was eating me up inside. The thought of being happy did not exist in my mind and it was a feeling I never believed I would have again. It took many years to be able to recover from the heartache and sadness, and to finally be in a better place. There is nothing more beautiful than when you prove to yourself how strong you truly are.

I am speaking my truth and sharing my darkest days with you, and it definitely was not easy. However, I wanted to be completely transparent with my book in hopes that any of my lessons can help anyone in some way. The lessons I learned were priceless, it helped me, and I am continuing to grow. Through all the pain and suffering, all the tears that were shed, the long and sleepless nights that I cried myself to sleep waking up with swollen and puffy eyes, I can finally say that I get it. I understand why I endured all the pain.

I understand why I made all of those mistakes—I have learned so many great lessons it has shaped me into who I am today, and I am not sure if I would take any of it back. *If I never made those mistakes, how would I ever learn to make it right?* I am now stronger and I am better because of it all. I want to continue helping people find strength and hope in their adversity. My purpose in life is to help people move forward, to help them. Sometimes you must allow yourself to break down in order to build yourself back up. We are all a work in progress, but we must learn from our mistakes. Every mistake we make is a learning opportunity. Some lessons are harder than others....but if we can become better because of it then I would say it was all well worth it.

I get it. Sometimes we find it easier to hold on to things instead of sharing them. We choose to bury it deep inside our soul and to never think or speak on it again. It may be the natural thing for us to do. That may be how we were conditioned. We may think if we share that means we are opening up and letting people in. We may think we are exposing the pain and we are ashamed because of it, we may become humiliated about it and we do not want to be vulnerable and in full fear that people may be judging us.

We must try to remember that when we do share, we are allowing others an opportunity to learn and grow not from our mistakes but from our valuable lessons. Everyone goes through trials and tribulations, but one thing is for certain, we all have the power within us to get through whatever those challenges may be in life.

Sending love and light to all.

www.ingramcontent.com/pod-product-compliance
Lightning Source LLC
Chambersburg PA
CBHW052157110526
44591CB00012B/1978